I0764167

On Sleep and Sleeplessness

Aristotle's Theory of Rest, Dreams, and Consciousness

A Modern Translation

Adapted for the Contemporary Reader

Aristotle

Table of Contents

Preface - Message to the Reader

Rebuilding the Greatest Library in Human History

Thousands of years ago, the Library of Alexandria was the heart of global knowledge — a sanctuary where the wisdom of every known civilization was gathered and shared freely.

And then, it was lost.

Now, we're rebuilding it — and you are invited to join us.

At the Library of Alexandria, we've set out to make every book available to *every person on Earth* — not just in print, but in every language, every format, and for every reader.

Here's how we do it:

- **Deluxe Print Editions at True Printing Cost** - Order any book as a high-quality paperback, elegant hardcover, or stunning boxset — and only pay what it costs to print. No markups. No middlemen.
- **Unlimited Access to the Greatest Works** - Enjoy thousands of timeless classics — from Plato to Shakespeare to Tolstoy — in beautiful, modern eBook and audiobook editions. Read and listen without limits — for every reader, everywhere.
- **Modern Translations for Every Language & Dialect** - We're reimagining the classics in clear, accessible language — and translating them into every dialect imaginable. Everyone deserves to understand humanity's greatest ideas.

When you visit **LibraryofAlexandria.com**, you're not just accessing books — you're joining a global movement to restore, preserve, and share the wisdom of civilization.

Join us today at LibraryofAlexandria.com

Together, we'll ensure the light of human wisdom never fades again.

With gratitude,
The Modern Library of Alexandria Team

Visit:

www.libraryofalexandria.com

Or scan the code below:

Introduction

Ancient Greece was a civilization famous for its great contributions to philosophy, politics, art, and science. It thrived from the 8th century BCE until the Roman Empire started to decline. Greece's city-states, especially Athens, were the heart of culture and intellectual thought. This was the time when democracy began, impressive buildings like the Parthenon were built, and famous playwrights like Sophocles and Euripides produced their works. The Greeks' curiosity about the world around them laid the foundation for Western philosophy. Thinkers like Socrates, Plato, and later Aristotle, pushed the limits of what people understood about the world.

Greek society was deeply connected to theism, which focused on a large group of gods and goddesses who were believed to control every part of life. But this system did not prevent people from exploring new ideas. In fact, it coexisted with a growing interest in finding logical explanations for nature and human life. Intellectuals would often debate and discuss these ideas in public places like the Agora. Aristotle grew up in this dynamic environment, learning from earlier philosophers, and later challenging and expanding their ideas.

Aristotle's Life

Aristotle was born in 384 BCE in a small town called Stagira, located in northern Greece. His father, Nicomachus, was a doctor for King Amyntas of Macedon, and this allowed Aristotle to be around the Macedonian royal court from a young age. When his parents passed away, Aristotle was sent to Athens at the age of 17 to pursue his education. Athens was the center of intellectual life in Greece, and Aristotle joined Plato's Academy, which was the most respected school of the time. The Academy was a place where students discussed everything from ethics to science. Although Aristotle learned a lot from Plato, he did not always agree with him, especially when it came to metaphysics, which deals with the nature of reality.

After spending almost 20 years at the Academy, Aristotle left Athens around 347 BCE after Plato's death. He traveled around different cities in Greece, continuing to study and learn. In 343 BCE, he was invited to the court of King Philip II of Macedon, where he became the tutor of Philip's son, Alexander, who would later become known as Alexander the Great. Aristotle taught Alexander about philosophy, ethics, politics, and science. Aristotle's influence is visible in Alexander's leadership style, which showed respect for knowledge and strategic thinking.

After teaching Alexander, Aristotle returned to Athens in 335 BCE, where he opened his own school called the Lyceum. Unlike Plato's Academy, the Lyceum focused more on recording knowledge and observing nature. Aristotle and his students performed research, studied animals, and took notes on what they observed. The Lyceum became a major center of learning, and it rivaled Plato's Academy. This is also where Aristotle wrote many of his famous works.

Later in life, after the death of Alexander in 323 BCE, the political climate in Athens became difficult for Aristotle because of his connections to the Macedonian court. Accused of disrespecting the gods, Aristotle decided to leave Athens. He fled to Chalcis, where he passed away in 322 BCE. Even though he had to leave Athens, his legacy lived on through his many writings and the influence of his school, the Lyceum.

Aristotle's Impact on Western Thought

No figure looms larger over the development of Western philosophy and science than Aristotle. A student of Plato and tutor to Alexander the Great, he unified logic, ethics, politics, rhetoric, and metaphysics into a coherent system that shaped intellectual inquiry for centuries. Although his writings reflect the best knowledge of his era, they also reveal a distinctive way of understanding the world—one that balances observation with rigorous logical analysis. Over time, this method has profoundly influenced everything from political theory to modern scientific methodology.

Aristotle approached knowledge as an interconnected whole, seeing each field of study as a vital path toward truth. While many earlier thinkers focused on abstract concepts, he emphasized direct observation of the natural world. By systematically examining and classifying what he saw, Aristotle laid the groundwork for the empirical methods now central to modern science. Although our understanding of nature has evolved, his legacy endures in today's emphasis on evidence-based research.

Logic: The Foundation of Rational Inquiry

Often hailed as the "father of formal logic," Aristotle introduced a system of reasoning that shaped intellectual discourse for over two millennia. In works like the Organon, he analyzed how valid conclusions are drawn from premises and introduced syllogisms—deductive arguments that became standard tools in philosophy, theology, and science. Even contemporary logic, despite its modern mathematical and symbolic advancements, can trace many of its core principles back to Aristotle's pioneering analyses.

Metaphysics: Exploring the Nature of Reality

Aristotle's Metaphysics offered one of the earliest comprehensive explorations of existence at its most fundamental level. There, he described the nature of "being qua being" and introduced the concepts of potentiality and actuality to explain how things change and develop. These ideas deeply influenced medieval scholastics—both Christian and Islamic—who integrated Aristotelian reasoning into their theological frameworks. Today, discussions about consciousness, identity, and free will still reference these Aristotelian notions.

Ethics and the Pursuit of the Good Life

In the Nicomachean Ethics, Aristotle proposed that the ultimate aim of human life is eudaimonia, often translated as "happiness" or "flourishing." He argued that we achieve this through virtue, developed by cultivating good habits guided by reason. His famous Doctrine of the Mean asserts that moral virtue resides between two extremes—for instance, courage lies between recklessness and cowardice. This focus on character formation has profoundly shaped the tradition known as "virtue ethics," influencing modern debates on moral education, personal development, and what it means to live well.

Politics: The Role of the Individual in the City-State

Aristotle's practical approach to ethics naturally extended into political theory. In Politics, he explored various forms of government—monarchy, aristocracy, oligarchy, democracy—and weighed their merits and pitfalls. For Aristotle, a well-ordered polis (city-state) exists not merely for survival or trade but to enable its citizens to live virtuous, fulfilling lives. His conviction that ethics and politics are intertwined remains influential, informing contemporary discussions on citizenship, governance, and justice.

Rhetoric: The Art of Persuasion

In his treatise Rhetoric, Aristotle examined how persuasion works, detailing how arguments must appeal to ethos (credibility), pathos (emotion), and logos (logic). This clear framework for effective communication continues to guide public speakers, legal advocates, and writers. From ancient courtroom orations to modern political campaigns, Aristotelian rhetoric underpins many of the strategies people use to sway audiences and shape public opinion.

Beyond these core subjects, Aristotle made significant contributions to biology, physics, psychology, and aesthetics. In the Poetics, for example, he investigated why humans respond so powerfully to tragic drama, pioneering the concept of catharsis—the emotional release that audiences feel through art. Throughout the medieval period, thinkers like Thomas Aquinas integrated Aristotle's theories into Christian theology, while Islamic philosophers such as Avicenna and Averroes preserved, interpreted, and expanded upon his works.

Across centuries of reinterpretation and debate, Aristotle remains a living voice in contemporary thought. His insistence on systematically gathering evidence and connecting it to logical principles laid the foundation for what we now recognize as the scientific method. His inquiries into human flourishing, civic responsibility, and the nature of argument continue to spark discussion and inspire new research. From personal ethics to societal organization, Aristotle's ideas help us frame enduring questions about how best to live, learn, and understand reality.

In sum, Aristotle stands as a foundational pillar of Western thought. He bridged abstract theorizing and practical inquiry, bequeathing a vision of knowledge that values both reason and experience. From ethics and politics to science and art, his ideas have been woven into countless intellectual traditions. Even today, as we grapple with questions of morality, governance, and truth, we walk in the footsteps of an ancient thinker whose breadth of insight and depth of analysis continue to guide our pursuit of wisdom.

Final Thoughts

By preserving Aristotle's legacy, we protect the intellectual depth and rigor that defined his way of understanding the world. His systematic way of asking questions, his classification of knowledge, and his ethical theories are still relevant today, providing a model for critical thinking across many subjects. This preservation is important not just for philosophy students but for anyone interested in the foundations of human thought and the development of ideas that shape the world we live in.

One of the difficulties in studying Aristotle's work is that his ideas and language are complex. Translating these works into our modern language is a key step in making his profound insights easier for more people to understand. By putting his ideas into today's language, more readers can engage with his thoughts, even if they don't have a background in classical studies. Making Aristotle's work accessible means adapting them to modern ways of thinking without losing their original depth. This helps bridge the gap between ancient and modern readers, making sure Aristotle's work stays relevant.

On Sleep and Sleeplessness

When it comes to sleep and waking, we need to look at what they are: whether they belong to the soul, the body, or both; and if it's both, then what part of the soul or body they involve. We also need to find out why animals have sleep and waking, and whether all animals experience both, or if some only sleep, others only wake, or if some do neither or both.

Additionally, we need to ask what a dream is and why people sometimes dream and sometimes don't. Or maybe people always dream but don't always remember their dreams. If that's the case, we need to explain why that happens.

Another question is whether it's possible to predict the future in dreams, and if it is possible, how does it work? Also, if it's possible, does it only apply to things people will do, or also to things caused by nature, chance, or higher powers?

First, it's clear that waking and sleeping involve the same part of an animal because they are opposites, and sleep is just the absence of waking. We know that opposites, in nature and everything else, happen to the same subject. For example, health and sickness, beauty and ugliness, strength and weakness, sight and blindness, hearing and deafness—all of these happen to the same being. We can understand this better by considering how we know when someone is awake or asleep. We assume that someone who is sensing something is awake, and everyone who is awake either notices something happening outside them or feels something within themselves. So, if waking means using your senses, then it makes sense that the same organ that lets animals sense things is also what allows them to wake up or sleep.

But since sensing things isn't something that only the soul or body can do, and since sensing is a process where the soul works through the body, we can say that sensing isn't just something that happens to the soul. A body without a soul can't sense things either. So, sleep and waking don't belong to pure intelligence or lifeless bodies.

Now, we've already divided the parts of the soul before. The part that takes in nutrition can exist by itself in all living things, but none of the other parts can exist without it. This shows that sleep and waking don't happen in living things that only grow and decay, like plants. Plants don't have the ability to sense things, even if that ability can exist separately from other things. In its potential and relationships, it can be separate.

It's also clear that no animal is always awake or always asleep; both of these happen alternately in the same animals. If an animal doesn't have the ability to sense things, it can't sleep or wake up, since both sleep and waking are based on the activity of the main sense organ. It's also impossible for an animal to always be asleep or always awake because every organ that has a natural function loses its strength if it works longer than it's supposed to. For example, eyes stop working after seeing for too long, and the same happens with hands and any other part that has a job to do. If sense perception is the job of a special organ, and if this organ keeps working past its limit, it will lose its power and stop working. So, if being awake is when sense perception is working, and if some opposites can't exist at the same time while others can, then since waking and sleeping are opposites, one of them must always be present in an animal. It follows that sleep is necessary. Finally, if sleep is a state of powerlessness caused by too much waking, and if too much waking can sometimes be unhealthy, then powerlessness or loss of activity can also be healthy or unhealthy. This means that any creature that wakes up must also be able to sleep because it can't keep using its powers forever.

In the same way, no animal can always be asleep. Sleep is something that happens to the sense organ; it ties up or stops it from working. So, every creature that sleeps must have the ability to sense things. Only something that can sense things can sleep, but you can't use this ability while you're asleep. That means that everything that sleeps must also be able to wake up. We can clearly see that most animals sleep, whether they live in water, air, or on land. Fish, mollusks, and all other creatures with eyes have been observed sleeping. Creatures with hard eyes and insects show signs of sleeping, but their sleep is so short that it's hard to tell if they're really sleeping or not. On the other hand, we don't have clear evidence that shellfish sleep, but if the reasoning we've followed is convincing, we can agree that they do.

So, based on these points, we can conclude that all animals sleep. We define animals by their ability to sense things, and sleep is a kind of pause or break in sense perception, while waking up is the release or loosening of this break. Plants don't have these experiences because without sense perception, there is no sleeping or waking. But creatures that have sense perception also feel pain and pleasure, and those that feel these things also have desire. Plants don't experience any of these things. A sign of this is that the part of the body responsible for nutrition works better when the animal is asleep than when it's awake. Nutrition and growth happen more easily during sleep, which means that animals don't need sense perception to help with these processes.

Now, we need to figure out what causes sleep and waking, and which sense or senses are involved in these experiences. Some animals have all the senses, while others don't have them all. For example, some animals don't have sight, but all animals have touch and taste, except for those that are underdeveloped, which we've talked about in another work on the soul. Since an animal can't use any of its senses while asleep, sleep must involve all the senses at once. If sleep only affected one sense and not the others, then the animal could still sense things while sleeping, which is impossible.

Each sense has something unique, but they also share something in common. For example, seeing belongs to sight, hearing belongs to hearing, and so on. But all senses share a common power that lets us know when we are seeing or hearing. For sure, we don't use sight alone to know that we are seeing, and we don't use just taste or sight to understand that sweet things are different from white things. This understanding comes from a common ability that connects all the senses. This common ability is linked most closely to touch, because touch can exist without the other senses, but none of the other senses can exist without touch, as we've discussed before in our studies of the soul. Therefore, sleep and waking must involve this common and controlling sense organ. That's why sleep and waking happen in all animals, because all animals share the sense of touch.

If sleep were caused by something happening to each of the senses individually, it would be strange that all the senses, which don't always work at the same time, would stop working at the same time. You would expect the opposite, that they wouldn't all stop working together. But according to the explanation I've just given, everything makes sense. When the organ that controls all the senses, and to which all the others are connected, is affected, then it makes sense that all the others are affected at the same time. But if just one of the connected senses stops working, it doesn't necessarily mean the controlling organ will stop working too.

It's clear from many examples that sleep doesn't just mean the special senses aren't working, or that we aren't using them. That's what happens when someone faints. A faint is when the senses stop working, and other situations of unconsciousness are similar. People who have pressure on their neck blood vessels lose feeling and become unconscious. But sleep happens when this inability to use the senses doesn't come from an accident or outside cause, but when it comes from the main organ responsible for perceiving things. When this organ loses power, all the other senses also lose power. But when one of the special senses loses power, the main organ doesn't necessarily lose power too.

Next, we need to explain the cause and nature of this experience. There are different types of causes (final, efficient, material, and formal). First, we say that Nature works toward an end, and that end is good. Every creature that can move but can't move continuously needs rest. Rest is good for it. Based on experience, people compare sleep to rest, which makes sense because sleep is rest from the effort of using the senses. Sleep helps keep animals alive. But being awake is the best state for an animal because using the senses or thinking is the highest goal for any being with those abilities. These abilities are the best, and the highest goal is what's best. This means sleep is necessary for every animal. By "necessary," I mean that if an animal is going to exist and have its nature, it must have certain abilities. And if it has these abilities, it must have others as well as a condition for having the first ones.

The next thing we need to talk about is the kind of movement or activity happening inside the body that causes sleep and waking in animals. The causes of this in all animals must be the same or similar to those in animals with blood. The causes in animals with blood are the same as those in humans, so we need to study this based on examples from humans and other animals with blood. We've already decided in another work that sense perception in animals comes from the same part of the body that causes movement. This part is one of three specific areas, and it's located between the head and the stomach. In animals with blood, this part is the heart, because all animals with blood have a heart. From the heart comes both movement and control of sense perception. It's clear that movement, like breathing and cooling, starts there. Nature has designed both breathing animals and those that cool themselves with moisture to conserve the heat in this part of the body. We'll talk more about cooling later. In bloodless animals and insects, which don't breathe, the "natural spirit" puffs up and shrinks back down in the part of their body that's like the heart in animals with blood. This is easy to see in insects with undivided wings, like wasps and bees, and also in flies and other similar creatures. To move or do anything requires strength, and holding one's breath creates strength in animals that breathe. In those that don't breathe, the strength comes from holding in the natural spirit. That's why insects with undivided wings make a humming sound when they move. This sound is caused by the natural spirit rubbing against the diaphragm. Movement in any animal involves some kind of sense perception, whether it's internal or external, and it happens in the main sense organ. Since sleep and waking are experiences of this organ, the place where sleep and waking start is clear—it's where movement and sense perception begin, which is the heart.

Some people move in their sleep and do many things just like they would when awake, but they don't do this without some kind of dream or sensory experience. A dream is like a sense impression in a way, but we will talk about dreams later. Why is it that people remember their dreams when they wake up, but don't remember the things they did while asleep? We've already explained this in the book "Of Problems."

The next thing we need to consider is: What are the processes that cause waking and sleeping, and where do they come from? Since animals need to sense things in order to take in food and grow, and since in animals with blood, food turns into blood, or in animals without blood, it turns into something like blood, we must look at the veins, which hold the blood. The heart is where these veins begin, as shown by anatomy. So, when food enters the parts of the body made to receive it, the evaporation from the food enters the veins, changes, and turns into blood, which then moves toward the heart. We talked about this when we discussed nutrition, but now we need to repeat it so we can understand the beginning of this process and figure out what happens to the main organ of sense-perception that causes waking and sleep. As we've seen, sleep isn't just any lack of sensing. After all, unconsciousness, certain kinds of choking, and fainting also cause a lack of sensing. It's also a fact that some people in deep trances still have an active imagination. This creates a problem because, if someone could faint and then fall asleep while fainting, we might think the image they see in their mind is a dream. People in deep trances, who were thought to be dead, often say things while in that state. However, all of these cases should be considered as something other than sleeping or dreaming.

As we said earlier, sleep doesn't happen just because someone can't sense things; it happens because of the evaporation caused by digesting food. This evaporated matter moves to a certain point, then comes back, and changes direction, like a tide flowing through a narrow strait. In every animal, heat naturally moves upward, but once it reaches the upper parts of the body and cools, it turns back and moves downward in a mass. This is why people get sleepy after meals. The matter that moves up, both liquid and solid, is heavy in large amounts after eating. When this matter stops moving, it makes a person feel heavy and causes them to nod off. But when it moves downward and pushes the heat down, sleep comes on, and the person falls asleep. This is confirmed by the things that cause sleep. Whether it's something you drink or eat—like poppy, mandrake, wine, or darnel—all of these cause a heaviness in the head. People who are sleepy and nodding off seem to be weighed down because they can't lift their head or open their eyes. Sleep is especially common after meals because the evaporation from the food is plentiful then. Sleep can also follow certain kinds of tiredness because fatigue weakens the body, and the dissolved matter works like undigested food. Some illnesses have the same effect, especially those caused by moist and hot fluids, like fevers or lethargy. Young children also sleep a lot because all their food is carried upward. You can see this in how their upper bodies grow bigger than their lower bodies when they're babies, since growth happens more in the upper parts. This is also why children are prone to seizures, because sleep is similar to epilepsy and can be considered a type of seizure. That's why many people have their first seizure while sleeping, and their future seizures happen during sleep, not while they're awake. When the heated evaporation moves upward and then comes down again, it stretches the veins and squeezes the passage that allows breathing. This explains why wine isn't good for babies or their nurses (it doesn't matter if the baby drinks it or the nurse), and they should only drink it diluted with water and in small amounts. Wine has a lot of heat, and dark wine even more so than other kinds. The upper parts of babies are so filled with food that they don't even lift their heads in the first five months after birth. It's similar to people who are very drunk, where a lot of moisture rises in their bodies. It's also reasonable to think that this is why embryos remain still in the womb early on. As a general rule, people with small veins, dwarfs, and those with large heads tend to sleep a lot. For people with small veins, it's hard for moisture to flow through them. For dwarfs and those with large heads, the evaporation moves upward too quickly. On the other hand, people with large veins don't sleep as much because the moisture flows easily through their veins, unless something else affects them and blocks the flow. People with a lot of dark bile also don't sleep much because their internal organs are cooled, and the amount of evaporation isn't very large. That's why they tend to eat a lot but stay thin, because their bodies don't seem to get much benefit from the food they eat. The dark bile is naturally cold, and it cools the digestive system and other parts of the body where it is present.

So, from everything we've said, it's clear that sleep is a kind of gathering or pulling back of heat into the body's center, caused by the reasons mentioned earlier. That's why people who are about to fall asleep often move around restlessly. But as the heat in the upper and outer parts of the body starts to fade, they cool down, and that cooling makes their eyelids droop. During sleep, the outer and upper parts of the body are cool, but the inner and lower parts, like the feet and the inside of the body, are warm.

But we might wonder why sleep comes on so strongly after meals, even though food and drinks like wine are warm, and sleep is caused by cooling. How can sleep be a cooling process if the things that cause it are warm? The answer might be that just as the stomach is warm when it's empty and gets cooler when filled with food, the same happens in the head when the evaporation rises there. Or maybe it's like how people feel a cold shiver when hot water is poured on them. When the warm evaporation rises, the cold rushes to meet it and cools it down, forcing the heat to retreat. Also, when a lot of food is eaten, the heat that carries the evaporation upward is like a fire that cools when more logs are added until the food is digested.

As we mentioned earlier, sleep happens when the matter that is carried upward by the heat moves into the veins and goes toward the head. But when too much of this matter rises and can't keep going upward, it pushes the heat back down and flows downward. That's why people tend to fall down into sleep when the heat that helps keep them standing (since humans are the only naturally upright animals) is pushed back. When this happens, they lose consciousness and then experience dreams.

Or maybe the answers we've given don't fully explain the cooling process. Instead, the brain, or the part of the body that acts like a brain in creatures without one, may be the main cause. The brain is the coolest part of the body. Just as the sun turns moisture into vapor, and that vapor cools as it rises into the upper atmosphere and turns back into water, the same thing happens with the evaporation from food. When the evaporation is carried upward by the heat to the brain, it cools and turns into phlegm, which explains why mucus often comes from the head. The healthy evaporation, which is good for the body, cools the heat when it returns downward. The narrowness of the veins around the brain helps keep the brain cool and stops too much evaporation from reaching it. This explains how cooling happens, even though the evaporation is very hot.

A person wakes up when digestion is done, and the heat that was gathered together in one place spreads out again. At the same time, the thicker, heavier blood is separated from the finer, purer blood. The purest blood is in the head, while the thickest, most impure blood is in the lower parts of the body. The source of all blood is the heart, as we've said here and elsewhere. The central chamber of the heart connects to two other chambers. Each of these chambers is connected to one of the two main blood vessels: the "great" vessel and the "aorta." The separation of the blood happens in the central chamber. However, going into more detail about this belongs in a different discussion. After food has been digested and the pure blood has gone to the upper parts of the body while the thick blood goes to the lower parts, animals wake up, free from the heaviness caused by eating. We've now explained what causes sleep: it's the pulling back of the body's matter, moved by heat, toward the main sense organ. We've also shown what sleep is, as it shuts down the main sense organ and makes it unable to function. Sleep happens out of necessity because it's impossible for an animal to survive without the things that make it an animal, and rest is needed to keep animals alive.

The End

Thank you for Reading

You've Just Read a Piece of the Greatest Library Ever Rebuilt

Thank you for reading.

This book is one of thousands we're restoring, reimagining, and translating as part of the **Modern Library of Alexandria** — a global movement to preserve and share humanity's most important ideas.

What was once lost to fire and time is now rising again — not just as memory, but as living, breathing knowledge, freely accessible to all.

What You Can Do Next:

- **Keep Reading.**

  Discover more legendary works — in beautiful print, audiobook, or digital form — at LibraryofAlexandria.com.

- **Build Your Own Library.**

  Every title is available as a paperback, hardcover, or collectible boxset — at true printing cost. Craft a personal library worthy of display.

- **Spread the Light.**

  Share this book. Tell others about the movement. Help us translate every timeless work into every language, so no reader is ever left behind.

By finishing this book, you've already taken part in something extraordinary.

Join us at LibraryofAlexandria.com

Together, we're rebuilding the greatest library the world has ever known.

With appreciation,
The Modern Library of Alexandria Team

Visit:

www.libraryofalexandria.com

Or scan the code below:

www.ingramcontent.com/pod-product-compliance
Lightning Source LLC
La Vergne TN
LVHW041942100826
845152LV00003B/59

* 9 7 8 1 8 0 4 2 1 3 8 8 9 *